FEMINIST FRIGHT

Manual for Superior Men

A complete theory based on Einstein physics, Political Psychology, Systems Theory and Archetypal Psychiatry.

FORMULA

All success attraction
All disease obstruction
All recovery elimination

You must fast on all three
OBSTRUCTIONS:

People
Habit
Food

FEMINIST FRIGHT

If you're too accessible they'll make your life miserable. God was with me as I endured my hard lessons to overcome. How else to learn how mean, spiteful, status-driven, competitive, catty and cruel females have become? I had to endure, but from my own sisters, are you kidding me? That's the hardest lessons of life, unfortunately. I finally understood what men do: life is a war so keep out problems not invite in more.

HANGOUT CULTURE

WE GOTTA MAKE FRIENDS?
THE HIDEOUS IMAGE OF LONELY
HANGOUT HELL
RESISTANCE BUILT MUSCLE
DELUSIONAL WOMEN
CRY FOR ATTENTION
FURIOUS WOMEN/NICE MEN
EASY AND FLABBY
CAN'T BE TAKEN SERIOUSLY
THE LEVERAGE METER
CLUELESS WITH ROCKS FOR BRAINS
ATTENTION SEEKING
WALK THE STREETS IN THONGS
SOCIAL MEDIA AND WOMEN
COVERT NARCISSIST FEMALES
FAKE PEOPLE AND THEIR IMAGE
THE CURSE OF TOLERANCE
ACCEPTANCE PROLONGS HURT
MEN WANT SEX AND FOOD

HANGOUT CULTURE

If the #1 obstruction to our goals is people, then to succeed being alone is all you have to do.

I had to write 120 books to prove it was **THEM** not me just like an Indian in white man's country.

Why blood relatives? Because they're the ones we know. Being hateful people it's anyone close.

WE GOTTA MAKE FRIENDS?

All everyone ever told me is I have to "make friends" and I always fell short cuz I just wanted isolation.

How can I make friends if I feel sick around them and can't relate in any way nor trust em?

I was always too busy going inside to make friends. I never ever thought about it in fact, eh.

How can you **FOCUS** and win on a project if lotsa friends are always calling to hangout for a bit?

Why make friends when my inner realm was like a multimillion window cornucopia without em?

THE HIDEOUS IMAGE OF LONELY

Yet they make us feel like we wear a **HIDEOUS** image of utter loneliness and inferiority don't they.

A friend is one who helps you to your goals man, not a nuisance, a bad influence or a distraction.

They came over to do what you do cuz they're too cheap or undomestic to do those same things Sue.

HANGOUT CULTURE

You've got your home so nicely set up those cheap and undomestic souls wanna come and hangout.

HANGOUT HELL

Every time they call & you meekly accept you're very disappointed having made other plans, eh?

Don't let em use you for entertainment cuz you're the one who affords it. Don't let em/they're twits!

Every time you'd prefer solitude instead but you're bit by the "social bug" making you feel real big, eh.

It takes time, dedication and FOCUS to be a winner inventor of whatever. That means alone sir.

A narcissist is never done with you. They think they own you so will be back when you're up Sue.

Watch out cuz the moment they get access to you the cycle will kick in again & you'll be screwed.

Early life may have been tribulation but actually that was preparation: one builds the other son.

RESISTANCE BUILT MUSCLE

You needed that dialectic, that resistance to build social muscle. This will overcome all obstacles.

You needed to suffer with people to know what to be and what to avoid, how to discern good/evil.

To all the Trump haters: You're nuts, he has said nothing wrong--you're just dam liberals that's all.

Is it me that is the problem or y'all that is the problem? That's how I looked at the human system.

HANGOUT CULTURE

A 12 year old heard a rumor about a woman and killed her. Elder disrespect never happened before.

The biggest red flag is a woman influenced by her friends more than her husband: bedlam!

Women seek divorce cuz a friend got one. Their social group determines how they think hon'.

DELUSIONAL WOMEN

Paranoid, delusional, backward & touchy: this is the modern female who actually knows nothing.

Look at Whoopi and Joy, the longest viewed TV of delusional liberal ladies sure to annoy.

Women will pay to have their patriot husbands labeled paranoid psychotic when they're the lunatic.

Women have become degenerates by definition. They know nothing, are carnal & just want attention.

The natural female is empathic concern for others while the "me" generation made them adulterers.

Female narcissists are more disgusting than males cuz they're so far from true female au naturale.

Degenerate females have sex on the first date and think nothing of it-- liberated, it makes em first rate.

CRY FOR ATTENTION

The modern cry for attention is degenerate since the superior female is supposed to be giving it.

Degenerate females bring their own house down: it's greener pastures not staying with one.

HANGOUT CULTURE

Degenerate females are more outer-oriented than attending to their home and ordering it.

Men are giving up on women but also women who can't find girl friends. Many women see the trend.

Women who fight these words haven't been stabbed in the back by a Jezebel or her spirit in them all.

FURIOUS WOMEN/NICE MEN

It's just a sign of the times when women are furious and men are becoming increasingly more sheepish.

Female murders are up tho' too, as their mouth makes men mad and they too lost self-control Sue.

Some may have your best interests at heart, but many don't who say they do. Women are liars too.

The minute she gets a leg up she'll take over and always she'll ghost you just when you need her.

If you can find a lil' old lady from the past, hold onto her for dear life cuz it's a dying generation, aye.

They're backwards but touchy when you mention it. They give **VERY BAD ADVICE** while lovin' it.

I've seen frenemy old ladies give advice sure to ruin a girl's life. Did they know? I think so, aye.

HOW MANY of your "friends" have you best interest at heart, and how do you know their true part?

EASY AND FLABBY

They've become easy and flabby. Having no morals they'll sleep with a best friend's husband see.

HANGOUT CULTURE

A nice lady is not offended by these words. She herself being chosen has been the target of girls.

They don't know why: they just hate you for being different. This is like a jungle degenerate.

Like Whoopi, if you don't think like them you're their mortal enemy and war is declared, amen!

They follow what a friend said & look at where it led when a judge didn't give as was expected!

They're used to listening to their girl friends, not to him. He's beginning to seem like a pariah to them.

CAN'T BE TAKEN SERIOUSLY

No superior man is gonna take these women seriously and as they age, vain fears sprout suddenly.

Her girlfriends don't seem strange tho' they are. It's her husband who's the nut in that reality [outer].

Her friends coach on how to get more money out of him or take control in some other way, hidden.

Any spoken problem brings immediate collusion of the other women & hell on earth for man has began.

They'll instruct how to screw him, how to get the most femalecentric lawyer who knows how to do it.

THE LEVERAGE METER

With people like that your "leverage meter" is all. When you lose that they'll purposely bring your fall.

It's your actions determining whether you're degenerate or not. Are they vain, sensual and debauched?

HANGOUT CULTURE

What has happened to women when even women don't like em? It's especially scary with children.

As a girl you may have potential but you've lost for good now if he sees degeneracy like the crowd.

A loser can't be trusted cuza his actions--because he's a reckless crazy individual and a sick soul.

No one knew what she'd do next. She was an empty shell and a bag of bad news, a witch's hex.

There's no substance or stability, there is nothing. It's a degenerate, a lost cause and perishing.

CLUELESS WITH ROCKS FOR BRAINS

Clueless with rocks for brains. Girls, good men don't want that so find a husband/come outa the rain.

That's why it's so important women listen to MEN. Not a degenerate but those caring about them.

They don't wanna see you happier than them. In this generation we gotta hide it from our "friends"

If a woman has a boyfriend and she's seeking attention from other men that is CHEATING friend.

Modern women are attention-seekers [the red carpet] and this is horrible for a boyfriend: see it.

It is natural for a woman to love the charges in her circle but not to be a fame whore on things virtual.

In reality the desire for fame and fortune is a natural outcome of abandonment for more than some.

To have been put down constantly propels a compensatory device to prove yourself see.

HANGOUT CULTURE

Men should want healthy women. The weak/sick ones are attention seeking usually not real lovin'.

ATTENTION SEEKING

In the old west [true Americana] the attention-seeking women were in the bars, sparkly whores.

Men should want a woman who will order the home, fix perfect meals, spend time with y'all alone.

But that makes women mad when you say that. They want NO demands from men, just fads.

You're a dam dummy with a nice man but still attention-seeker. It's a bummer & you'll pay the piper.

Truth: most men give their women PLENTY but when it comes to attention it's never enough see.

They also seek attention to keep their guy in line, make him feel dispensable and disposable, aye.

A relationship is exclusive or get out of it. He cuts off other females, you do the same with men sis.

Female attention seeking combined with virtue signaling is where it really gets disgusting.

WALK THE STREETS IN THONGS

Girls if you wanna walk the streets in a thong or nothing on go ahead but ladies have honor with lads.

We swam in muddy waters so we ALL went wrong. Forget all that now, go on ahead reborn.

She's attracted to you but talks to a load of other men and doesn't even attempt to stop it man.

HANGOUT CULTURE

So many men know her it's not even funny. You think they didn't have sex--EVER--in their history?

I'm from the old school. I like men separated from women at my parties, I find it exciting.

The men smoke cigars in the library while the women group up doing their thing like gossiping.

Not gossiping but "discussing human relationships" which are none of their business, that's it.

SOCIAL MEDIA AND WOMEN

Social media has ruined women of all kinds. It's made em more attention seeking and even unkind.

You get this B.S. "friends are everything" since that's their way of being [not individuating].

They're operating out of illusion--a spell. That's why there's no common sense to it/it's hell.

Once they get close to you they run their games and slowly & insidiously your value's trashed ok.

I'd rather be alone than have my peace stirred up. That's a chosen one who has finally had it.

Chosen ones want authentic relationships while the herd man is looking to control: that's it.

COVERT NARCISSIST FEMALES

Look at the modern covert narcissist female out there. Now make a business decision about her.

They're not the illusion that they cast and all things fade away especially the fake self they display.

HANGOUT CULTURE

They should just keep their mouth shut but they don't know that due to the Dunning-Kruger effect.

When you start to better yourself you see who your friends are. You also see that in the gutter.

Fake friends wanna ride on your coat tails on the way up but disown you when down, that's well known.

Instead, get into the cycle of nature. I was blue in the social, standing out & triggering the impure.

FAKE PEOPLE AND THEIR IMAGE

They're fake people worried about an image, not wanting to be true & very nervous about you.

They don't wanna get close cuz your light exposes them. They RUN from you so just understand it son.

The less friends you have now the more popular later: it's like a tsunami after isolation of the clever.

How to conquer a country: get to their women first, for without them the men weaken like a curse.

Turn women against men and conquering the country is a given cuz so much energy is wasted in it.

In the same way women are anti-strong men they are Trump haters with TDS so bad it's pathetic sir.

You can't bankrupt a man just for beating Biden in the polls. What a great day for America after all.

It's a hard lesson to learn it but you won't have to again go thru it so forget it and enjoy each minute.

The weak spread themselves around. Both men and women lack discipline and boundaries hon'

HANGOUT CULTURE

THE CURSE OF TOLERANCE

If you're gonna take him at his worst, why would he ever change? He won't and you're cursed.

If he DOES change he will dump the one who tolerated him and find a different, whole woman.

You accepted him when he acted like trash and now he's well he wants a woman with panache.

He's trying to live his life and become a better person but you had no real standards nor reason!

Ladies, be careful what you tolerate. Cuz when he's ready to commit he's won't respect it ok.

Ladies, be careful what you tolerate. Cuz when he's ready to commit he won't respect you ok.

It's disgusting when a woman puts herself down to accommodate a cheater or a poor provider.

ACCEPTANCE PROLONGS HURT

Whatever you accept you'll get more of it. Nip it in the bud or jolt him awake before ever marrying it.

Rule # 1: Dating is not about sex. It's about getting to know the person kinda like he's on probation.

You don't just jump in bed with someone and then get to know em as you go along: that's all wrong.

The best advice is: If you want a relationship be celibate and never be embarrassed about it.

Saying it another way, if you want to have something lasting you need to close your legs ok.

HANGOUT CULTURE

Women must hold off on sex until sure he cares about them and his WORDS are irrelevant ma'am.

Men know the words "I love you" are the open-sesame keys. Hold you head up high & don't let this be.

MEN WANT SEX AND FOOD

Men are motivated by two things in life: sex and food. They'll tell you anything when in the mood.

When you've given him sex you've given your treasure with no more to offer lest you're wealthier.

"He's a diamond in the rough but I can mold him. I can make him be what I want cuz I love him."

Men wouldn't cheat if women weren't so careless with their bodies so blame them too ladies.

A false preacher says "God loves you unconditionally" and the laity thinks: I don't have to repent see.

Since governments tend to get more power son, every generation has to fight for it's freedom.

FEMINIST FRIGHT

HIDDEN SIBLING ABUSE
MALICIOUS SISTER ABUSE
THE DEPTH OF BETRAYAL TRAUMA
YOU ALWAYS HAVE OPTIONS OR WILL SOON
SUCCUMBING TO FAMILY MYTHOLOGY
FALSE CHRISTIAN BRETHREN/SISTERS
MS. SOCIAL CHARM & NARCISSIST MAN
MAKING CLOWNS INTO KINGS
WOMEN ARE CRUEL TO EACH OTHER
AVOID JEALOUS MAIDS
NARCISSISTIC HOOVERING
COMING BACK WITH WORSE DEMONS
PTSD: GETTING ILL FROM MEMORY
DEATH ROW CONVERSIONS
CROWDED COUNTRIES ARE CATASTROPHE
INTELLECTUALS BANNED FROM GROUPS
NARCISSISTIC ARROGANCE
UNTENDER FEMALE POLITICIANS
FEMALE FLYING MONKEY ATTACKS
A CELL IS BETTER THAN A CROWD
FEMINIST POLICE STATE
FAIR SPEECH IS UNFREE
EXHILARATED ACCUSATIONS
NO TALKING HER OUT OF IT
FEMINISTS DEFINE REALITY
SPEAKING TRUTH GETS YOU FIRED
WONDERFUL WOMEN BIGOTRY
JEZEBEL MICHELLE
LIBERAL "LOVERS OF PEOPLE"

FEMINIST FRIGHT

NEVER PAY TILL THE JOB IS DON
NEVER LET EM BACK IN
CARNALITY IN A FALLEN ERA
MATURITY IS BEING ABLE TO WAIT
DIVORCED FROM DRUMBEAT
SEXUAL LIBERATION WAS DOOM
OPEN BORDERS CHURCH ADVOCATES
HEARKEN: CHURCHES FALLEN
DIVERSITY KILLS MERITOCRACY
FALSE CHURCH "INTELLECTUALS"
LATTER DAYS ARE FILLED WITH VIOLENCE
THERE IS NO SOCIAL ANXIETY ONLY BOREDOM
WHY SHOULD I GET USED TO IT
FALSE CHRISTIAN EMERGENT CHURCHES
HIGHEST PRIVILEGE: WESTERN CIVILIZATION
ELDERING CONSCIOUSNESS
AGE OF MULTI-IDENTITIES/POSSIBILITIES: COLLAPSE
ACCEPTING LIBERALISM IS YOUR MORAL DECLINE
ALPHA MEN STAND *AGAINST*
MARRIAGE IS A FENCE
MODERN MOVIES ARE PROPOGANDA
THE AUTOIMMUNE PROTOCOL FOR SENSITIVES
PROTEIN NOT FROM EGGS AND DAIRY
MICRONUTRIENTS IN [DANGEROUS] GREENS
BACON AND SALMON EASIER TO EAT
FEMALE MANAGES LOVELY HOMELIFE
FASTING VS. BACON ARGUMENTS
THE VISCIOUS VEIL OF VEGANISM
GREENS: OXALATES, GOITROGENS, LECTINS

FEMINIST FRIGHT

People: If you're too accessible they'll make your life miserable.

In a moral religious generation females become sisters, in an immoral era they become bitter warriors.

HIDDEN SIBLING ABUSE

That's exactly what those demons would say. Taking the most innocent thing and twisting it ok.

Why am I a prolific writer? Having been silenced for decades of sister abuse I exploded later.

When the covert schemes of siblings to harm us blew up in their face we humbly looked away.

They aim to hurt anyone who speaks up/breaks the silence on the extent & depth of the abuse.

It was all a mobbing mentality: WE think this and WE think that excluding the black sheep brat.

The mobbing mentality is what makes them SEEM so right and you SEEM so wrong, all alone.

It wasn't these people it was an evil force in the world they embodied due to social hypnotism.

Just accept those people are gone forever and get others. There's only One God however.

FEMINIST FRIGHT

MALICIOUS SISTER ABUSE

The siblings, nieces, nephews and even extended family are all complicit in this leviathan python.

That's why we go no-contact with every blasted one of em. They were all part of the put-down.

You walk into a room and all hate you but you know none of em--but your sister does hon'

Out of pure malicious hatred and envy your sister has been reputation-killing for decades honey.

It hurts--it really hurts--the precious lesson that: blood is NOT thicker than water, fact.

It hurts when siblings are the enemies, doing everything to keep you from what is yours rightly.

But when you face facts/get educated on it you're ready for this serious blow, preventing trauma.

THE DEPTH OF BETRAYAL TRAUMA

A betrayal felt so deep I fell mute for years too scared to make a peep but then got educated see.

Cain and Abel--first stories in bible--were on sibling envy and murder, of this I'm ever mindful.

Even recovered victims-turned trauma therapists show extreme bitterness when discussing this.

They can't get over it totally and have it in their craw till they die, that's the depth of treachery.

We come in alone and go out alone--those ties are broken with our passing but feel everlasting.

FEMINIST FRIGHT

Born clear we come into a unique system awaiting us then it takes decades getting over this.

Who else would they be jealous of? Their own sibling is there for the taking for supply or targeting.

YOU ALWAYS HAVE OPTIONS OR WILL SOON

You always have options to take back your sanity, peace of mind and ambitions, in a minute.

If they've punished you for setting healthy boundaries or speaking up, God sees/laughs at the chumps.

The underhanded things they did went not unseen and in the end God takes care of everything.

Never forget God sees everything and everyone reaps what they sow eventually, now proceed.

We choose to release these unhealthy players because it is like a POISON for scapegoat empaths.

She ruined every relationship I had that she knew about. Smart separation ended all that.

Unreported, hidden, denied, malicious/criminal sister abuse is opening the eyes of millions too.

And we won't stop talking cuz it's our therapy telling all what happened when silenced see.

Sibling abuse becomes criminal when trust funds and inheritances are messed with ya' know.

SUCCUMBING TO FAMILY MYTHOLOGY

We can't assume just because they're part of a family they're safe, loving, kind or gentle see.

FEMINIST FRIGHT

Amazing healing, trauma recovery, awakening to the truth, miracles occurring, happiness too.

Did you have toxic siblings/did their covert schemes backfire as you escaped from liars?

We don't need revenge now that we're happy, successful and living out our highest pursuits.

All these years we thought they were friends, could be counted on were trustworthy are gone.

Typically there's more than one in a family: one parent and one sibling seething with jealousy.

Christian siblings so "uplifting" but in reality they're gaslighting, accusing, triangulating, rejecting.

Basically the siblings are covert spies as you catch them over and again in their web of lies.

FALSE CHRISTIAN BRETHREN/SISTERS

The Christian sibling listened to the smear campaign of some gay guy over her sister's testimony.

Cuz the gay guy was social and the scapegoat was not they accepted his smear without thought.

Christians ignoring the good book and going with society's kooks instead: false brethren.

You can't be a Christian and walk in step with society's false narratives and accepting all of it.

False brethren/sisters will always go with whoever's socially acceptable or high on the totem pole.

He has more money, he rules the family: that is baloney to me especially if involving sociopathy.

FEMINIST FRIGHT

Miss Shit: You are lowminded with no talent/no self-discipline just forcing the fit, arrogant.

Since sodomism portrays homosexuality as superior they will always take the gay guy's smear.

MS. SOCIAL CHARM & NARCISSIST MAN

She's Ms. Social Charm, knowing how to work it. I don't so am powerless in the social hypnotic setup.

Jealousy. I'm not saying you're jealous but that it's a dominant force in the world around us.

So he can get another housekeeper/live in whore. You start your new good life of success galore.

Shame-breaker: If she can't cheer you on it's a false brethren and you're better off without em.

MAKING CLOWNS INTO KINGS

He's just a loser who makes stuff up as he goes and never follows thru with what he says.

Living with an unstable man is like living on quicksand and you don't need it, vet em carefully.

Instead of caving into an adrenalin flood over shame, always relabel it: "on me this was laid."

Are you waiting to be discovered or still hidden under God's hand? When He lifts it, sudden fame.

They turned blooming flowers and a lovely garden into disgusting, rotted, moldy weeds and poison.

Start pulling the weeds one by one and you'll feel your freedom coming back. To white from black.

FEMINIST FRIGHT

Instantly you start having more discernment and wisdom, feeling liberated from the dumb.

You'll feel liberated from neurotic gangland cuz that's what a sick system is man, a sad prison.

WOMEN ARE CRUEL TO EACH OTHER

They're not use to seeing women do better so when she does they block/degrade/gossip about her.

Women are cruel to each other, the major triggers being looks and age. Stay home with husband ok?

Every person who blocked/tried to ruin me was a woman and they are brutal but it's all explainable.

Diminishing opportunities, lost sex appeal and can't get a man: It's sad and that's why they do that.

They can be so cruel to each other it's beyond comprehension. I can still remember it man.

Small liberal towns are most treacherous because you're expected to be social and they own you.

The worst family setup is the Cinderella Syndrome where two older sisters always outvote/demote her.

It's always two against one, triangulation-strangulation. And they love being insidiously devious hon'.

God said "sorry for putting you through all that but it's the only way you'd learn cuz you wouldn't listen".

If she has a maid the maid will shrewdly bring her down, humiliate her somehow, call her old.

Being a Queen is difficult, you must balance psychological forces like this but knowledge is **POWER** sis.

FEMINIST FRIGHT

AVOID JEALOUS MAIDS

A woman has a jealous maid and falls into depression, paranoia, resentment, anger and trembling.

I do all housework myself--anything to not have a women around! There's no house big enough son.

Not only do they drop hints of your obsolescence they gossip about everything they see in a house.

One way or another they'll get something from you so your piece of the pie doesn't lessen them.

We're competing for men, I guess that's the reason for this hostility and it's archetypal/universal see.

Don't self-deprecate cuz a woman scorned you. Think what the likely reason is--she's jealous Sue.

She lacks what you got: a husband or home or clothes or good looks or countless other reasons to hate.

Many women hated me just for being different. They hate novelty cuz they've been made to conform see.

Whenever they ask you to do something for the good of the group rather than the self, it's communism.

Your piece of the pie takes it away from them, that's how they think. We think infinity, they think lack see.

The minute you sense ageism withdraw immediately. You don't deserve denigration but respect see.

A woman's weapon is gossip and calumny: reputation murder. In many cases this can be the worst.

Rely on husband for protection from women. This is the smartest course so keep things good with him.

FEMINIST FRIGHT

A husband and home is freedom from the world which imposes it's nastiness constantly and it's deadly.

It's too bad I couldn't get to know you better but intersex suspicions intervened and now it's over.

You say it was only one word! Yes but that one word indicated deeper levels of disrespect, worlds.

The crap older women tolerate dealing with projections, we don't need any more headaches hon'.

They'd clench their teeth with seething hatred for me, all cuz I was a threat to their status in society.

NARCISSISTIC HOOVERING

Any narcissist makes you feel like you are owned by that person, even way later when they hoover.

Allowing that spirit back in is a curse, always brings more demons with it worse than the first.

Let him/her back into your life and the next situation is always way worse than the first of course.

Every time I gave her another chance she was compelled to destroy me in a worse way than before.

"I know it's been awhile but you're always on my heart" then you're used until they're bored.

"I know it's been awhile but you're always on my heart" then you're used 'til they're bored, discarded.

A narcissist will use you for a season but they will always discard you again. Avoid this, Christian!

COMING BACK WITH WORSE DEMONS

FEMINIST FRIGHT

I forgot how I went thru hell getting rid of her/him the last time or I figured they had grown outa crime.

I had to get an eviction notice and countless other hoops jumped through but later let her come here.

After an eviction notice and countless other hoops jumped thru I let her back in to my doom.

Whenever they leave they return with seven demons worse than themselves, what a mess.

Let this be a lesson miss, carefully vet everyone who comes in esp. around your kids and pets.

Hoovering is how the narcissist manipulates you into breaking no-contact, a dangerous fact.

HOOVER OF EGOS BRUISED

So why do they hoover, Sue? Because you successfully went no contact and their ego's bruised.

He thinks after all: "She put ME down, she got rid of ME?" She can't do that, that's not narcissist feed.

Let em back in, prepare for a slaughter. I couldn't believe who she brought with her, a hatchet murderer.

Honey, they don't love you they just need to control you. It's the human element and it's trouble.

She'll do little things to annoy or sadden you. She'll leave the gate open so your precious pets go thru.

A twisted demonic self-esteem is anchored in controlling you so it's narcissistic injury when you're thru.

It's not they don't want you they just don't want anyone else with you so it's very dangerous too.

FEMINIST FRIGHT

If you leave and start a new relationship they'll do anything to break it up THEN they'll move on.

They need you for support, sex, money. They left you for others but see you're better supply honey.

They'll bring evil gossip, talking to others about you then coming back to give you the blues too.

When they moved on you heard nothing from em cuz they had better supply. It's all about that honey.

Now they're in a position where they need that thing only YOU supplied so prepare to say goodbye.

From beautiful to ugly: That has to be a demon when someone changes that fast/ages overnight.

The point of hoovering is to regain that sense of control over you NOT BECAUSE THEY WANT YOU.

PTSD: GETTING ILL FROM MEMORY

We're the only species who gets mentally ill from its memories. First we're calm then we're crazy.

Crisis avoided but another one looms. Until we go home again that's human growth and evolution.

Their attacks are deliberate/socially accepted cuz they have power while your attacks are reactive.

You're an ageist and it's very boring. I'm at the top of my game but you put me down due to aging?

There's a strain in men's movement that hates women. They mock, demean and throw em bones.

Weak men do deliberately cruel things to shit-test women: drop em off in other cities and leave em.

FEMINIST FRIGHT

I don't like women either but being on the receiving end is not good my friend I need a Christian man.

I don't mock and demean women cuz they're vermin but cuz their cruel bitches if they're liberal.

After all, they believe in abortion don't they? They leave their nice husbands and kids, don't they?

I take solace in the fact that when we're dead all memory is gone too--none of this hullaballoo.

DEATH ROW CONVERSIONS

Men on death row who are so smart, evolved and well-spoken: man has two sides/they were broken.

The best saints WERE the worst sinners. Man has two sides--in everyone there's a tiger inside.

The severe degradation/finality of being on death row triggers the other side/banishes all pride.

Once you spiral down to the bottom it's "been there done that" and you're now a mature man not a rat.

There are 2 separate nervous systems, 2 brains [left and right] and TWO states [saved/damned].

The worst becomes the best, the best becomes the worst and nothing stays the same so stay on course.

I'm a lady, you're a gentleman but if you get adversarial I will rebel and articulate it man.

This is COOL: You've been screwed, you know how it feels when THEY/society sides against you.

In lectures to the public dirty jokes are allowed but saying whatever it is they don't want is fouled.

They'll allow you to be a sex sinner cuz then you're controlled but not self-aware and bold.

DON'T quibble over words ever again. NEVER debate with the turds it's futile and never-ending.

Female rulers start wars far more than their male counterparts--that alone says an incredible lot.

CROWDED COUNTRIES ARE CATASTROPHE
[FEMINISTS WANTING OPEN BORDERS]

Cruel, cold, unempathic, arrogant, groupy, complacent, hypnotized with luxury: this is [open boders] AOC.

Anyone who's lived in a crowded country knows how deranged it is to want open borders see.

Crowded countries are loud/dirty/chaotic. There is NO privacy, you see & smell things you shouldn't.

In crowded countries there's never enough resources so they all get hyper-competitive and clannish.

In crowded countries government is all-powerful and distant, not caring what you think one bit.

Cruel, cold, unempathic, arrogant, groupy, complacent, hypnotized with luxury: get away from me.

In crowded communist countries the rulers are rich and they plant lightning rods like AOC the witch.

They're good looking & charismatic, planting evil seeds and false narratives that are ridiculous.

Does your city have a pro-crime activist as a district attorney? If so, why in hell are you staying?

INTELLECTUALS BANNED FROM GROUPS

FEMINIST FRIGHT

If you're too intellectual you'll be banned from the group. If posts are too deep they're gone immediately.

I thought you were my friend but now I see you as my worst enemy. That's how it goes sweetie.

I lost all assertiveness in '92 when disagreement brought violence. Even the women got pugnacious.

Here I took the side of men and they turned against me for being a woman. Hmmm, not good hon'.

All through the decades of dung God kept sayin': put up with this and later you'll write it out telling all.

God said "you'll tell the world what people do to each other to hold em down in disease/the dumps."

Everything had to be filtered thru him, and how boring. Now I feel so free as I can just perceive reality.

I'm not comin' back cuz I'm too dam happy without you. I can say what I want and enjoy the day too.

If my light can't be hid under a bushel why not wait for God to push me thru? See I don't need you.

All those years in the dry lonely desert I stored up strength by putting brakes on it [constraint].

I waited and wondered envisioning the bright future tho' in a tiny cabin with a bike and not much more.

I never wrote in the dry years while on the Potter's wheel. I waited for God's spout gushing to reveal.

NARCISSISTIC ARROGANCE

All I saw was arrogance of the narcissistic devil claiming all knowledge originated with him/go to hell.

FEMINIST FRIGHT

The world wants empty accomplishments one after another so to WAIT makes you look a loser.

I didn't wait intentionally, I couldn't write. My head was a mush--the "fertile anarchy" preceding discovery.

What I had to go through to write this shit for you was unbelievable but it's ok/all worth it now.

I know what it's like to have a feminist/dominating mother and a docile/beta father--you're a loser.

To WRITE, learn to WAIT. Wait for the pearl don't push mediocre crap just to say you accomplished it.

Without that strong male influence while cowering before a narcissistic goddess archetype--OUCH.

UNTENDER FEMALE POLITICIANS

People naturally assume female politicians bring tenderness to politics but they DO NOT.

They make up crap conforming to the narrative and politics becomes ridiculous nonsense.

The femalecentricity of everything has become sickening. They act all-loving but are always scheming.

You had your chance and now I'm onto a new dance. You've changed so much too, not a prince.

Ten years of writing 18 hours a day took forty years of waiting, learning, storing up strength, crying.

Miracle maker: The stuff I put up with like a sheep to the slaughter in order to write about it all later.

After being around you I've chosen the side of good and decent for the rest of my life, no strife.

FEMINIST FRIGHT

A true writer is automatic after storing up strength and not writing just learning usually thru hurting.

FEMALE FLYING MONKEY ATTACKS

Don't let her in she'll ruin your life thru her flying monkey attacks based on her jealousies: fact.

Don't let her in she'll get all her friends against you as she fancies herself a female gang-leader too.

I was too zombified to cry so I just put up with impositions getting more extreme daily, that's my PTSD.

For the first time in my life I'm not adapting to other people and I'm so prolific in open schedule.

What a joy: fence/locked gate so you can't get to me plus the Grand Canyon divides us, goodbye creeps.

It was far worse than a tiny jail cell having to adapt to crowds of people, a cell's my monastery.

I'm sick of you, you're too puerile. Repetitive too or wrong stressors for narcissistic reasons in a dark soul.

So you know this guy and that guy, always name dropping. You think we don't see faking?

At fifty got a note from my sister about how it's too late and I was a failure-- that's the ageist liberal.

You're always gonna do this/gonna do that and frankly we're sick of hearing about it so just do it.

I was young and foolish, didn't know what I was doing. We pay for the rest of life remembering.

I wanna help people but mostly I want protection from them. Gotta have that to do the other, amen.

FEMINIST FRIGHT

A CELL IS BETTER THAN A CROWD

They all bothered me constantly til I thought I'd go crazy and I'd welcome a lonely/tiny cell believe me.

They wouldn't leave me alone--they were jealous of my privacy, of my independence and victory.

When you invade my office I can't do what I want. I can't move here and there without explaining it.

When you remember that crap with them on your back it's with you as a victim of inferiors--stop that.

Remorse: There is never true memory just magnetisms of the moment anyway so forget it honey.

You drove me crazy saying I drove you crazy, always accusing me of what you did everyday.

Think about this: Did they cast you out due to badness or your superiority making them jealous?

I wasn't writing anything ever, I just suffered and that triggered such deep levels I prospered.

Adult child of alcoholic says: "I'm sorry but I didn't know what to do. Who the hell knows what to do?"

Never feel bad when used to do God's work in punishing someone tho' you didn't know it at the time.

If you show weakness the sharks will circle. In the female community it becomes calumnious and brutal.

Another paradox is how feminists hate women wearing make-up but it's ok when a man wears it.

If stuck in a trauma bond the most attractive man is the one who might hurt you/is dangerous too.

37

FEMINIST FRIGHT

FEMINIST POLICE STATE

It's a feminist police state on campuses. The boys are afraid to say anything, no jokes/never catcalls.

A small group gained control of the knowledge base of "what we know" about gender male and female.

WHY aren't feminists fighting for women's rights in other countries? They bitcthin' about trifles, so silly.

If you disagree with feminists they call you evil/giving them PTSD--giving them license to hurt, see?

They get back by doing the same things they say we're doing: demonize, objectify, "otherize".

Feminists don't hesitate to be rude, snarky and MEAN. There's so much meanness defending "victims".

The spurious scholarship is obvious as "experts" repeat factoids, untruths, rumors, exaggerations.

It's sympathy research about how oppressed women were then they went off the deep end called "science".

The feminists are literally given the power to make a federal case out of their mis-perceptions.

Politicized scholarship is NOT a consistent body of work. They need to debate and hear from dissidents.

So sick of hearing about the patriarchal male hegemony when women had it so good in this country.

NEW JARGON LIKE "WEIGHTISM"

It's ALL on the negative impact of "WEIGHTISM" on women--not of dangerous obesity on them.

FEMINIST FRIGHT

There are blurred lines between legit science and social justice activism, can hardly tell the difference.

Feminist fat-positivity movement even wants to make obesity research illegal--it "increases stigma".

Every time you do something you didn't want to do it builds character, endurance, self-worth.

FAIR SPEECH IS UNFREE

It's no longer "free speech" but rather "fair speech" and the definitions of that are with the observer.

Feelings have become the new measurement of human rights and it's all about the supposedly victimized.

Marketplace of IDEAS has been replaced with the marketplace of OUTRAGE, far more insidious.

Cuz feminism is about intersectionality, it won't criticize honor killings since it would be against Islam.

Third wave feminism is identity politics, it is authoritarian and it is interventionist--it is ONLY Hix Politix.

With PTSD the memories are very fresh--they jump out at you and become more horrendous with age too.

Every time you don't go back you're building self-worth. Every time you give in increases the curse.

Just say "NO!" then turn. This opens up your internal worlds of creativity and joy--no more hurt.

With age there's more depth of emotional response--we can't believe it while before denial blunted this.

We can't fall apart when it happens, we must prepare the bruised emotions to battle the memories/demons.

FEMINIST FRIGHT

The vulnerable mind locks onto something which becomes a possessive force from then on.

Rather than marriage being protection for females, it was now seen as confinement by tyrant males.

Microaggression: unintentional slight hurting someone-while the intention of the speaker is irrelevant.

Owners of companies intimidated by their own engineers coming from Stanford etc: snowflake culture.

Feminists feel EXHILARATED rebelling against the oppressive patriarchy by their own stories.

EXHILARATED ACCUSATIONS

The feminist can silence a room by telling her victim story which fits right into the liberal audience's narrative.

It's all anecdotal, their victim story referring to another victim's story to confirm the false accusation.

It gives her a real rush to accuse others of not being sensitive enough or "educated" about this stuff.

She's speaking on behalf of the suffering by God, and you're just an insensitive fool, a bigot.

We all wanna feel "good" and what we're doing matters but what's wrong here is their arrogance.

It makes them feel so courageous, speaking about this dominant male oppression all through history.

She's powerful: when she speaks as a "lesbian woman of color" a hush falls on the room, what valor.

The self-identified woman has incredible authority since NO one in the room dares contradict her, oh my.

FEMINIST FRIGHT

Once she feels the power of false accusation who wouldn't claim it save those repelled by it?

It's a sincerely held belief that this is the way the world is. They won't allow YOU to shake it--IT JUST IS.

NO TALKING HER OUT OF IT

To be talked out of it would be to surrender her righteousness in her struggle against oppression.

By me trying to explain the world to her, I'm then "siding with the oppressors" and worthy of censure.

She must continue believing her position tho' shown to be false. That's why your debates are futile/endless.

Take a conservative view of anything and she says "you deny my right to exist" and she persists.

You're denying my identity--which is my RIGHT to exist--and this keeps broadening in hicks politics.

They come up with things like micro-aggressions and unconscious bias that can't ever be measured!

Systemic bias or unconscious oppression is why more women aren't in physics, that's their position.

To them it's so pleasurable to be a radical. A heady rush: in God's universal eyes they're the apple.

It's a combination of euphoric rage in heady self-righteous indignation and explosive outrage.

The power to define reality is the greatest power one can have, and feminism has it. Dr. Fiamengo

But they can't hold onto the conviction in the context of their western upbringing and happy family.

It is reported that after 911 professors showed pleasure at what happened to America--haters of goodness.

To get normal people to see something wrong with normal sex was the feminist goal. Janice Fiamengo

FEMINISTS DEFINE REALITY

As women continue to define reality men will be rendered near voiceless both privately and publicly.

If one has not swallowed the feminist cool aid they are not even allowed to ask non-feminist questions.

Why is one lonely dissenting voice so intolerable to these feminist women who are such great "scholars"?

Men are being punished for offending feminist women. These gals call his work reporting the vermin.

Feminism degrades through intersectionality: concerns with racism, ableism, transgenderism, Islamaphobia.

These feminists are useful allies ONLY if they promote intersectional doctrines irrelevant to feminine.

Feminism also must show deference to those who claim greater victimization/marginalization than they.

SPEAKING TRUTH GETS YOU FIRED

If you say white man got job thru privilege, ok. If you say black man got it thru affirmative action, you're fired.

If they're gonna talk about "bias" how about the bias which continuously works in women's favor?

All money goes to encouraging women or searching out naysayers against the current feminist line.

42

FEMINIST FRIGHT

In a competitive world we ALL feel we must prove ourselves--how does that show bias?

Perhaps women feel they must prove themselves because they haven't yet proven themselves?

Perhaps women feel questioned because they deserve to be questioned, not take their truth for granted?

In this era of affirmative action pressures to hire women, those hired are not "top notch", no question.

WONDERFUL WOMEN BIGOTRY

Feminism depends on an image of the angelic nature of ALL womanhood while ALL men are hoods. START

It's called gynophilia: the COMPULSION to see women as always good no matter what they did.

The culture has great difficulty in recognizing female aggression and cruelty: an unseen tragedy.

They can't conceive of female evil at all--Jezebel: Even as it stares us in the face we can't be appalled.

The warped view says women never act from "badness" just innocence warped by prejudice and abuse.

Women can peddle any degree of Wonderful Women Bigotry and never be seen as contradiction.

JEZEBEL MICHELLE

They invade, they take. They come without calling, they rape. Whatever you have they want it, ok?

Satan and these losers are the "sucking spirit". Anything you have and anyone you know should fear it.

FEMINIST FRIGHT

She wanted my cosmetics, I gave em to her. She wanted my clothes, ok here. She invaded more: goodbye forever.

Stop blaming Jezebel Michelle for her actions and instead blame yourself for ever letting her in.

Stop blaming Jezebel for her actions and instead turn it around to all the times you did the same things.

For the sinner is GRASPING just as he is miserly. He snatches everything in sight and is totally disorderly.

Sorry for what you went thru learning about evil people. Had you not been sheltered you wouldn't need to.

LIBERAL "LOVERS OF PEOPLE"

Liberals are "lovers of the people" saying they're all good/you should let em all in though it's over for you.

If you put all this into a bag called SUCKING SPIRIT it will make it all evident so you can now ignore it.

The sucking spirit will take, TAKE, take until you stop it, ok? "Bottomless pit" is Satan's other name.

Jezebel is compelled to test your limits when under her spell. Tormented, "peace at any price" I yelled.

When the weak woman feels rejected she can become sadistic as she gets others to swing the hatchet.

Especially the SLUT--being filled with spirits from men and all their contacts-- is a irksome haunted house.

The grasping sucking spirit is blind to it's own beastly actions--there's no humanity left in the heathen.

Once she finds a sucker she'll milk em 'til he's dry: that's you until you'd had enough and drew that line.

Worse yet, she'll take your man--anything you have and then some! If not, she'll borrow money from him.

Use the Jezebel Sucking Spirit for all your discernments. You will be protected and happy if you do this.

NEVER PAY TILL THE JOB IS DONE

You never pay until the job is done, and you never say it's done if it isn't. Be happy, learn from mistakes.

Women: never let Jezebel fakes into your married life. Keep her out of what's sacred or say good bye.

Women FIGHT WITH GOSSIP. That's their main tool--getting others against you to make you her fool.

Sad suckers forgive without repentance. Jezebel hasn't changed but you take her back in nevertheless.

In the sad generation everyone's on the take and it's all taken for granted as we sink in our swill together.

The Jezebel uses social psychology totally. She's on the phone destroying reputations constantly.

My God, girl--everyone is not your friend. You may want em to be but grow up woman, it's a WAR we're in.

NEVER LET EM BACK IN

Once the nightmare is over and she's gone, try to forget this cyclone. I know it's hard but you must to grow.

The amount of men taken in by the Jezebel spirit is inconceivable. Learn to discern humble from evil.

Once you come out of denial you REALIZE the social psychological upheaval brought on by foe Jezebel.

FEMINIST FRIGHT

She got everyone against you--the greatest tool in her arsenal and you had to endure this to learn it too.

She's got a big dam mouth and she's on that horn all day balancing factions around her shall we say.

Jezebel is such a hot stove to me I won't touch it and totally stay away. Seeking escape I left the state.

The old crones saw right through this bothersome user but it was so common I couldn't discern her.

Names have been changed to protect the sluts, users and losers.

JEZEBEL IS DISASTER WAITING TO HAPPEN

If you don't get Jezebel outa your life right now you're headed for sure disaster with a loose cannon I know.

Jezebel doesn't know what she's doing--it's all reflex in a demonic hex--but you do so make her your EX.

Stop ruminating over Jezebel's actions and start asking yourself why the hell she was given the chance.

Stop fretting over women and men so evil and start realizing it's principalities and powers of the devil.

You now know the predictable lines of the Jezebel spirit which is great wisdom as you know to avoid it.

Where self-esteem is missing losers flow in. Remember that now, and put the blame on you my son.

It's my house, I paid for it, I wanna be alone so don't move in on my home and get your own for a throne.

It's obvious what money gives you: protection from the elements, the world and pushy grasping people.

FEMINIST FRIGHT

They trip themselves up constantly immersed in diversity shove-downs while you're God's child, His own.

Constrain all thoughts to the home. The vegetable soup you're slowcooking, the dogs/cats, your husband.

CARNALITY IN A FALLEN ERA

He was predatory--that's why it hurt so much having him around: it was like a big black grabby cloud.

It's the same with the women--they always got something up their sleeve. They won't leave it alone, so leave.

They be bringing up crap to make you think of that in a constant battle staying on top with your own map.

They won't just leave ya' alone to think for a change, oh no they gotta bring stuff up to bash/disparage.

They bring sad stories of dogs/cats to ruin your mood--like as if the problem's solved by making you blue.

They won't shut up. On and on they go, terrified of silence ya know--hens going for recognition below.

MATURITY IS BEING ABLE TO WAIT

Patience is a fruit of the spirit that only grows under trial. That's why we went through all that, for style.

True promotion comes from God.

This morning upon awakening I felt a **NEW SEASON** and it was so obstruction-releasing I'm celebrating.

You plant the seed in one season, you wait, and you harvest in **ANOTHER** season--that's the regimen.

It's immature to expect harvest right away cuz that isn't how nature works: everything's in stages.

FEMINIST FRIGHT

Everyone who abused me died early. Hmmm, it's strange when I think they were only 35 and 55, truly.

God was with me all the way as i endured my lessons. They were hard ones but had to be learned to overcome.

How else would I learn how mean, spiteful, status-driven, competitive, catty and cruel they were? I had to endure.

But from my own sisters? Are you kidding me? That's one of the hardest lessons of life, unfortunately.

ASSUMING THEY'RE ALL GOOD

As a sheltered sweetheart I assumed all were good. I had to get hurt repeatedly then I finally understood.

I had to understand what the men do: that life is a war and you gotta keep OUT the gore not invite in more.

"My alcoholic mother colluded with my two feminist sisters against me" and thus began her period of insanity.

It was two decades not knowing who I am. The underpinning of identity was smashed, I had to begin again.

I built back up in a small cabin in the wilderness. I became defined by God, my pets and the elements.

I became immensely happy out there all alone--like rain on a tin roof and how it sounds. In a shack, imagine!

I was so happy in my lonely shack I didn't want to leave it the day Ray drove me to my mansion--that's a fact!

After a decade in the sticks I added cable TV--now the history channel educated me on the human tragedy.

DIVORCED FROM DRUMBEAT

FEMINIST FRIGHT

For decades I was in the wilderness, divorced from the cultural drumbeat, and thus can really see the creeps.

Had I stayed & adapted to the sick culture I woulda surely died drunk but instead God gave me an out.

Having come back to civilization I feel like a Martian but that's a miracle for a writer with plenty of gumption.

I see the sick culture in a whole different way than those who had to adapt to it unfortunately and tragically.

I was under the tyranny of a feminist mother and two haughty feminist sisters so I can commiserate, sir.

They didn't listen to me explain for a minute, just as no liberal will listen to any conservative though legitimate.

When people came I felt invasion into my small space. What they called social was boring/conformist.

When invaded by earthlings I felt annoyed, scared, resentful and it showed. That's a "hater", ya know.

When I got em to leave I'd take a deep breath and get even more walled up against the energy-thieves.

Marriage began my real life. Before then I was invaded but now I was fenced in, protected, loved as a wife.

Marriage began my true freedom. I could expand, learn, enlarge--free of outside forces of doom.

If only women could see how marriage is the TRUE FREEDOM and being single is being targeted, alone.

SEXUAL LIBERATION WAS DOOM

Not only young women pressured to have sex, its weird/perversions they must endure and don't resist.

It used to be "NO" was the default setting for premarital sex, giving women leverage/men acting best.

Now "YES" Is the default setting for sex--so a single woman must explain why NOT and it's a real hex.

A young girl must be strong enough to go against her entire generation on this and refuse sex as Miss Priss.

Why would anyone want to have sex with a stranger? It's inconceivable but the dorms are orgy-chasers.

In the old days women had an edge--leverage--as men had to mind manners or be slapped as scammers.

Not only young women pressured to have sex, it's weird/perversions they must endure more and more.

Because when there's no lines, where everything goes, Satan enters in and what happens HELL only knows.

Some women are promiscuous thinking it means liberated--inviting a man for dinner and sex: a scary spirit!

A man invited for dinner felt a scary spirit in the woman. That's how it feels with sexualized female vermin.

Why should a woman explain why she doesn't want to have sex with him? Sex is sacred/casual is disgusting.

OPEN BORDERS CHURCH ADVOCATES

Churches pimping open borders. They have big signs that read "Jesus was an immigrant"--these are fakers.

Churches used to be against communism but now they're for it tho' it's another name they're calling it.

Like all virtue-signaling fakes, the open borders advocates never think of us tho' our very lives are at stake.

FEMINIST FRIGHT

I liked the preacher til he started up with this openborder crap--that's a sign of a faker, we all know that.

How can a preacher want open borders--you mean the LEGALS immigrants go to the back? Preposterous.

When a man is tired of London he's tired of life. --Anonymous saying 240 years ago before this violence.

What I see are elites publicly preaching multicultural platitudes but privately upholding actual segregation.

You may get in but you're not getting in for long and you're going out. President Donald J. Trump.

FALLEN CHURCHES AND THE INVASION

THE CHURCHES HAVE FALLEN and they won't stand up as we go under judgment thru INVASION.

Fallen churches are the ones bringing the invasion IN: They're the ones for open borders while we're forsaken.

What mean-spirited treachery: our very own CHURCHES are the traitors destroying our lives daily.

TRAITORS: It's like someone's bringing a dozen people into your living room-- how would you like that?

One day you'll wake up to a whole new POPULATION of multitudes camping on your front lawn--amen?

Bring it home--what this mass invasion means to you, me, our traditions and superior principals hard-won.

We're desensitized early: seared conscience brings callousness characterizing the Latter Day mess.

The fallen churches have signs "Jesus was an Immigrant" to justify them bringing in an invasion.

FEMINIST FRIGHT

Now it's the MORMONS who hate Trump. Calling him wicked names, all of it. They'd want Hillary instead?

HEARKEN: CHURCHES FALLEN

Help, harken! The churches have fallen! Allowing female priests, lesbians, perverts to preach, anything.

And now these fallen churches are bringing in MASSIVE immigrants to take your place and muck up the works.

You go to most churches and they are CUM-BA-YAH all the way, boring, contrived, skits, hurray.

The church elites are making stuff up to keep you paying up cuz it's a business and Jesus is left out.

Joel Osteen and Joyce Meyers and motivational speakers with a Christian background, OK fine.

But true Christianity is about repentance and that's what brings the right-brain reward: fun and dance.

The churches have fallen and WOMEN rule em! That's why they have fallen, females create doctrinal ruin.

New Age stuff--that's what they're into. Cosmic, transpersonal, we're-all-one BS, pagan, mystical.

Women can't hold to the line doctrinally speaking. Some break thru the feminist haze, the genius Queens.

DIVERSITY KILLS MERITOCRACY

Someone writes a book and it takes off. Soon after it gathers a mob it becomes concretized into moral law.

They started this multicultural crap in the eighties and suddenly there was no more meritocracy just idiocy.

FEMINIST FRIGHT

I had great exposure to beauty, greatness and sublimity but then came the 80's of multicultural insanity.

All you need is diversity: That's the license for ignorance of the college audience, like it's all there is.

We're supposed to be exposed to the greatness of humankind in college but instead they get this garbage.

Instead of being happy about the glorious music they gave us, they're mad that Beethoven wasn't a woman.

RACE AND GENDER LIMITING/BRIBAL

RACE and GENDER is so limiting and tribal, yet feminists insist all failure is due to sexism--not true.

"Diversity Bureaucracies" in universities and all large corporations is a multibillion dollar industry.

It's in the interest of diversity bureaucrats to sow this idea of racism and sexism, they make a mint hon'

They virtue-signal and blow their own horn about standing up against America's bigotry--it is weakness/folly.

Leftists in charge love to look out over their diverse realm in noblesse oblige but it's a power trip I think.

The Diversity Racket is making a mint at it: creating division and amplifying it all over while massively stoking it.

In a time with diminishing interest in Classical it is irresponsible to inject identity politics and wreck it all.

Marie Curie needed no female role models to study radioactivity just a passion to understand the world.

The ideological imperatives of feminism are trumping the search for scientific truth and its dangerous too.

FEMINIST FRIGHT

We're supposed to be exposed to the great minds in human history but instead we get this trashy misery.

The way you get there--incredibly big--is to become incredibly small. Lesson by Mother Theresa for y'all.

FALSE CHURCH "INTELLECTUALS"

Jesus said when the devil speaks he speaks from his own resources because the Truth is not in him.

They depart from the faith giving heed to seducing spirits/doctrines of devils speaking lies without conscience.

In the Latter Days they BOAST, covetous self-lovers, trucebreakers, false accusers, despisers of good.

They have a form of godliness—seem lit up—but deny true Power of God: turn away from these snobs!

Simply put, in the Latter Days you can't trust anyone but God said we'd always have one good friend.

Mormons I've known allowed New Age crap to seep in. Reincarnation, astrology even abortion.

For a church to be viable it must go by the book. Progressives wanna debate details while Jesus is forsook.

Leftists in charge love to look out over their diverse realm in noblesse oblige but it's a power trip I think.

It's an emergent idea that ignorant students feel entitled to berate, demean and humiliate adults.

A church will grow fast if they drop Jesus, never mention sin/repentance or hell, or conjoin with Islam.

Madonna believes in gays and abortion and that's what makes you ugly at sixty--when the soul's lost direction.

FEMINIST FRIGHT

As things degenerate you can't escape and fall more into your own bag of devices to avoid anxiety/hate.

AOC's comparison of Hitler to Trump is lazy, ahistorical and cheap but what can we expect from these creeps?

Trump wouldn't say he's deporting millions unless he has something up his sleeve. Joyously, I believe!

Invoking the holocaust to score political points? There are no words for these ignorant/callous fakes.

LATTER DAYS ARE FILLED WITH VIOLENCE

Latter Days are filled with violence so get ready as this ramps up to incredible, awful, catastrophic things.

We had a big fight and it worked out great. --President Trump on the tariff deal with Mexico.

YouTube bans any historical analysis of liberal socialist, communist or left-wing anarchy applied to the present.

Leftist groups are Marxist power-mongers aiming to eradicate Western culture and European ethnic groups.

A system has two choices at one point: go into entropy (disorder, randomness) or realms of higher order.

The kids are the ones launching the New World Order through their disorder and then reactions to our horror.

Horror at disorder: that's what it was. A land where there is no justice, no logic, just debauchery and fans.

The liberals all wanna virtue-signal about reparations but when it comes to details they never discuss em.

With liberals everything is a gateway drug to something else as we continue to diminish.

FEMINIST FRIGHT

There were times when you were just pure instinct and a bundle of unintuitive behaviors, so forgive him/her.

THERE IS NO SOCIAL ANXIETY ONLY BOREDOM

In order to FIT you mal-adapt--go dead inside--and that's mistakingly called "recovery from social anxiety".

There is no "social anxiety" there is only boredom and sensing you're wasting your life with uncertainty.

The New Age church is androgynous: male unified with female, yin-yang is the whole thing and it's nuts.

I saw a gentle lamb become a raving bear and it was like a bomb hit my identity which had been so paired.

All men have two sides: higher and lower, good and bad, left vs. right, freely creative or obdurate.

There are two brains and two separate nervous systems--and the best becomes the worst and visa-versa.

Literally, the best saints were the worst sinners. it's a matter of direction energy takes: gutter or winner.

Immense energy creates or destroys. It's either creative self-expression or creative self-destruction.

The low-class gross can't hope but impose. They bring their friends, gossip and sleep on your porch.

The low-class gross are never satisfied. You give em something, they just want more and even despise.

To the dumb, social is the whole thing. Hanging out hides useless tendencies but they can still sting.

Jezebel Spirit is prevalent in women. If they have a friend they'll get their men friends to drag her down.

56

FEMINIST FRIGHT

It used to be Independence was the American spirit but now it's SOCIAL and it's so boring and irrelevant.

As a young child I was sickened that sociability was expected. I'm not a herd animal I am God's girl.

WHY SHOULD I GET USED TO IT

They say if you stay in the social it won't hurt so much but that's just mal-adaptation to the bunch.

Why would I wanna waste my time with your SEVERELY dumbed down atmosphere? Boring, weird.

There were times in history where they'd kill you for being different/set apart, the genius saints with a heart.

I invited her to partake of the wonderful solitude in the country and she brought half the town of loonies.

The crass, gross and loose inevitably impose. The gentile have restraint/easy to bear but Jezebel has lows.

They are LAX: loose, unregimented, disorderly, catty, unreliable and generally a loose canon--that's the rabble.

The gross are like roaring lions in a China shop and to have a happy life you gotta see this or good luck.

When a mental famine comes over the whole herd it's called a DROUGHT and it feels like a broken heart.

Quit virtue signaling about how nice people are. It's a people-worshipping generation/shut up dark heart.

I could be banned for putting people down. But did you know that was Mark Twain's greatest draw?

So what if they don't believe it/are too dumb to see it? That's irrelevant to a great sage you twit.

FEMINIST FRIGHT

She fights you with the strength of the herd behind her cuz you're independent--hanging out you don't prefer.

I didn't have a fence in Borrego, was invaded by the whole town. Even churches were social, the clowns.

The churches have FALLEN into social justice BS and communist thinking shifted to illegal immigrants.

They come to our country, scam our system and hate us but we can't say a thing or make a fuss.

Disgusting democrats go along with all debauchery. How can you possibly be involved, they're filthy.

FALSE CHRISTIAN EMERGENT CHURCHES

Thru false Christianity emergent churches have fallen into globalism but about citizens they could care less.

White liberals will pay a foreign man three times what the job's worth just to show they're not racist sir.

The reason I'm cranky is because you invaded my privacy. I'd be civil if you weren't such a downer pill.

Not only did you invade my privacy you brought your friends who were EVEN WORSE than you, amen.

The liberal atmosphere in college caused insanity, I mal-adapted all over the place but in solitude was ok.

Satan can make you a drunk or to hate your husband. Imagine all the troubles when marriages end.

Many women divorce their husbands only to become sluts. Both are "modern" but with aging it's nuts.

God didn't die on a cross so you could buy a new house or car--prosperity teachers miss the mark.

FEMINIST FRIGHT

He suffered the horror of the cross to keep us out of the horrors of hell: for days, suffering so horrible.

Modern lies: Everybody's good, everybody's the same, God loves em all and they're all goin' to heaven.

It's remarkable how when atheists die their last breath they call on GOD tho' all their lives they were mod.

The degree of maudlin caterwauling in universities over identity is impossible to overstate. Heather MacDonald

Identity politics is tearing our society apart.

Identity politics is teaching people to hate the great thinkers of the past and also their fellow Americans.

HIGHEST PRIVILEGE: WESTERN CIVILIZATION

The Universities should pass on the highest privilege: the vast inheritance of western civilization.

We must push back against the idea of systemic racism/sexism cuz that's the basis of victimhood narcissism.

They literally see everything as an existential threat to these "poor students", a direct result of the brainwash.

As long as the victimhood is in place you'll have demands to shut down "hate speech" and it'll get worse.

An unsurmountable obstacle or a cakewalk/turkey-shoot? The ground is so backward and you're so cute.

They're SO dense, hypnotized, out of order/divorced from nature and grace of COURSE you'll ace!

You're competing with great minds now but know you're the best at what you do/they can't compare to.

FEMINIST FRIGHT

You'll always win over an immoral competitor. Don't be impressed with their talents as much as their character.

It's my house, I paid for it, I wanna be alone so don't move in on my home and get your own throne.

Borego was just my bootcamp--I learned all my lessons from that. I've forgotten all of it and now I'm fab.

Due to feminism boys are discouraged early and that's why they have no confidence in abilities.

I am here to advance His kingdom. I came to take over not to fit in.

Feminism is being used to take out politicians we don't like and to change the culture radically.

How many more of the unwholesome pride parades must we witness to see it all as a debauched mess?

Not just my sister: she was my resistance-training, counter-force to overcome, the reason I work so hard.

ELDERING CONSCIOUSNESS

Eldering is a precious stage of life in the human experience. Body recedes while temporal lobes open to eternity.

Eldering: Don't bemoan it or suicide to escape it. It's the highest time in the human life, believe it.

Elders are superior but ruthlessly put-down in the West. Ignoring that is your test then come to your crest.

Because the ageist projections are so cruel and rude, most slide into lower archetypes of doom.

To know you're the highest as an elder you gotta know they're the WORST kinda character to cast you as a number.

FEMINIST FRIGHT

Women are very competitive and when they fail to find a flaw they will weaponize your age/call you old.

It's the little inflections, the raised eyebrows indicating youth is one-upping through the age thing.

You just gotta realize the cruel crap in an ageist society and learn how to avoid it, minimize it, transcend it.

You see their debaucheries, their callous/cold antipathies and their negligence so it's hard tolerating these.

The worst part is having to live with the younger generations. I don't know how you do it, I'd wanna run.

A loser who can't compete any other way will always pull the age card. It's disrespectful and low: discard.

Stepping away from politix and all their tricks. Return to real world of yard work, fixing soups, loving pups.

In my new stage I don't even care if I'm relevant. Chocolate, green soup, enjoy the day, yard work.

AGE OF MULTI-IDENTITIES/POSSIBILITIES: COLLAPSE

Multi-identities and possibilities is a sign we're on the verge of collapse. Gender games, masks, all of it.

A society that treats its unborn like medical waste is doomed. Paul Joseph Watson

The sovereignty of the INDIVIDUAL vs. identity politics which devolves to tribalism, anarchy, violence.

Find your own mind by looking out the window not searching exes on the internet or following politix.

PRIDE. That's my background of hard work, penury and good use of time-- dress, house, car is fine.

Losers live in another world. Everything is put off for the windfall, meanwhile the yard goes to hell.

It's sick and it's evil and I just wanna be free of y'all.

I needed love and when I got it felt totally protected. Free of losers invading me I could do what I wanted.

If they ever got into power they'd do anything to make us bend to the faddish trends of the socialist left.

ACCEPTING LIBERALISM IS YOUR MORAL DECLINE

There's a moral decline just by accepting liberalism then with stress there's a break into pure hedonism.

You need not explain to anybody why your way is better. Just the fact that she can't see it, forget her.

Don't be encumbered by your need to explain yourself. These disclaimers are a weakness and they know it.

If they were put down as kids that ol' ego takes off when given an edge and it can be dastardly I allege.

Giving the vote to teens is more dangerous than an atom bomb--talked into anything or bought off.

We moved away so she couldn't snipe from the wings or discombobulate our lives anymore and we soared.

The "peaceful" man is actually dodgy, avoidant, cowardly, indecisive, fence-straddling and milquetoast.

The milquetoast male lost his way. He turned from Jesus the ONLY way to study transpersonal psychology.

The milquetoast beta male is perfectly adapted socially/sees the truth in everything but don't trust him.

FEMINIST FRIGHT

Any man who would turn from the One True God to worship culture, books, and liberalism is inwardly flawed.

To reject the Master of the entire universe and destiny for a bunch of inferior documents worth a penny.

He underlined it all like it really meant something. And it all means nothing, it is trash compared to the King.

From what I experienced I must say: I hate the "male feminist" cuz compared to the common man he's a sadist.

ALPHA MEN STAND *AGAINST* THINGS

Just as carnivores seem to have a better connection with animal life, a real alpha male is gentler.

A man who **STANDS** for something and stands **AGAINST** things. My husband was a fence for me, I'm free.

When people are sweet like that they're really hiding a monster inside.

I endured waiting a month for your silly lackluster efforts but had to cut you loose when it was over.

You were a cloud without rain. There was **NOTHING** inside, just a nice exterior that never ever gave.

They're all clouds without rain. So once you find a reliable worker treat him like a king and hold on forever.

Once you find that worker who's a supple paint brush in your hands you've got it made/bring on the fans.

They're **ALL** clouds without rain. They smile, they pander, they promise and there is nothing ever to gain.

They say they can do it and know what you're talking about but that's just the Dunning Kruger Effect in mobs.

FEMINIST FRIGHT

The white race has the capacity to think deeply/abstractly at multi-levels of artistic production/DISCOVERY.

Every race has it's own genotype and this is ours, thanks. In other things they are better perhaps.

Some people just can't think deeply. It's not their fault certainly, it's from generations of inbreeding.

But that Dunning Kruger Effect of the dumb thinking they're smart will always tell you they can do the job.

Carving out your own way and INSISTING on it every single day marks your new life as a discoverer/frontier.

MARRIAGE IS A FENCE

I had to be imposed on so much that I finally exploded--by imploding to my own reality then I WALLED UP.

For I have a RIGHT to my own reality don't I? Not to them--they wanna control even your thoughts and attention.

ONLY marriage--not a convent--takes a woman outa of the rat race into her own queen domain, protected therein.

I got married and Ray got rid of all my faux friends and enemies alike. I was free, protected: he drew a line.

Marriage is like Big Daddy: he gets rid of the bullies. Women need that or they're marked/beholden to sharks.

The Dunning-Kruger Effect of thinking/saying they can do something when they can't--but I won't complain.

She was aghast I was disgusted with her. Blind in her denial, self-delusion and sin she called me a hater.

Liberals always blame others for what they are doing.

FEMINIST FRIGHT

No more entanglements with those you're outa sync with--think of that. A real vacation in the head.

The loser prefers self-destructive attacks rather than long-term trust built up from proving himself.

Because you're moral you're keeping them from doing what they want and they hate you for it--that explains it.

With online pornography it's a case of curiosity killing the cat--clickbate and all that, but watch this.

Husband controls the outside world and I don't wanna see anybody unless they wanna give me money.

Solitude--precious privacy--is more important than anything, every single minute and second in paradise.

Queen Elizabeth didn't touch Charles that much, he was like me far more comfortable with animals.

MODERN MOVIES ARE PROPOGANDA

Modern movies are filled with propaganda, are boring as "hell" with really stupid plots re: America.

Countless people will hate the New World Order and will die protesting it.
H.G. Wells

The American crisis started twenty years ago with control of public schools and dumbing down of kids.

We've been raising little Socialists for three generations, even grandma thinks like this--outrageous.

Trump is most loved and everyone knows it while they are left-wing activists disguised as journalists.

Doing evil in the name of justice is a very common theme in all socialist regimes and I see it in thee.

FEMINIST FRIGHT

Dumbed down, violent and entitled: Don't even try to talk to the brainwashed kids, everything has split.

Entitled, dumbed down, violent: They'll take everything you have because they deserve it.

If you're against the Green New Deal you obviously hate children, an uneducated redneck too dumb.

As FOX has become politically correct we all hate it, now with less conservatives than democrats.

THE AUTOIMMUNE PROTOCOL FOR SENSITIVES

As we age the declension comes in stages. An event happens, aging occurs and you don't go back, no sir.

The best way to avoid aging--skinny in your nineties--is micronutrients and phytochemicals e.g. KALE.

Not living on steaks but Old Lady Diet of smoothies, soups and salads from the best cuz you've studied it.

Smoothie: Bananas (cuz I don't count carbs/calories), berries, coconut, lotsa parsley and kale, water.

Gone are the days of nutbutter in my smoothie unless I wanna suffer all day from an autoimmune tragedy.

You cheated on pizza and heartburn almost killed you. NO: grains, dairy, nightshades, seeds or nuts.

You're different from them. You're a hypersensitive who can't eat stuff most are munchin' cuz you're above em.

Took me decades to get over the fruitarian nightmare cuz the micronutrients aren't there/deficiencies occur.

FEMINIST FRIGHT

It's in the greens, man. That's the most modern science and it's exact so why not take advantage of it?

PROTEIN NOT FROM EGGS AND DAIRY

Since autoimmune protocol says no dairy or eggs, you gotta get protein from fish or bacon today.

I just can't eat land animals, sorry. They are my friends and I know the fish are too but I gotta stay healthy.

It wasn't until I got to the AIP Autoimmune Protocol that food decisions became distinct and definite, so slick!

No wonder I was always sick as a child--allergic to dairy, grains, nightshades, citrus, seeds/nuts and eggs!

Paprika is used in practically all salad dressings and it is prohibited on the Autoimmune Protocol.

Restricting so many foods may seem impossible but how bad do you want to end your pains and get well?

Having recovered I'm all for the AIP Autoimmune Protocol in conjunction with Fuhrman's Nutritarianism.

Got a real rush from my PARSLEY and KALE in my smoothie this morning and it's a new life I'm adoring.

The fountain of youth is not in the orchards and vineyards but GREENHOUSES and what a rush, my gosh!

And what about nightshade cultures? Well they're passionate but angry and get real fat after thirty.

Orchards and vineyards of beautiful fruit is a refreshing treat and cleansing but these aren't the necessities!

Don't worry about dieting for if you have any pride, merely aging will propel you into it as you mirror it.

MICRONUTRIENTS IN [DANGEROUS] GREENS

Compared to the micro-nutrition in greens, fruit is just a pretty decoration on the table it seems.

Fuhrman says to EAT KALE it's highest in micronutrients while others say its the worst poison possible.

It's the anti-nutrients in greens that kill us slowly blogger says but another expert says they're the best.

I feel SO much better WITHOUT allergic foods (aforementioned) and WITH micro-nutrition & lovin' it.

What are the Z-bombs that eradicate a blight/make everything right? Greens, onions, mushrooms, berries.

Colorful fruits make great decorations/beautiful wall motifs but they aren't nutritious, that's in the leaves.

When I look at a person I think "will they be great at 60?" not how they look when they are twenty.

You can't take "medicine" or supplements to treat your nutritionally deficient diet. Sv3rige

Stop talking about supplementation and pharmaceuticals and start talking about diet: research and study it.

Seeking diet partner where we could discuss diet and experiment constantly, someone smart preferably.

I believe in the carnivore diet (beef/water/salt) but just can't bring myself to do it tho' life itself depends on it.

I don't LIKE the taste and texture of "grass fed beef". It tastes campy--like blood--and it's creepy.

BACON AND SALMON EASIER TO EAT

FEMINIST FRIGHT

When I think of eating lamb I picture a little lamb. No other food is gotten thru this kind of violence man.

So I guess you'd call me a "meat-abstainer" biblically. I think it's the gentler souls, hypersensitives.

It's not that meat-eaters vs. meat-abstainers are bad/sick but that there's two types of people I think.

I JUST CAN'T, IT MAKES ME SAD.

How do I get what I need to live if I don't eat meat? With autoimmune disease I'm allergic to everything.

Immune system attacks all food as an invader. Esophagael pain from acid-reaction to everything, man.

If I die this will be my last book. The reason will be: I never found correct diet or did but couldn't do it.

In the fifties everyone was skinny, men were handsome and the women pretty due to meal balancing.

They had salad, meat, vegetable, spud and even dessert and all were stunningly handsome, real flirts.

In the fifties when everyone was pretty people didn't diet. Eating just meat or just fruit would be criticized.

All that vegans do is try to hide the deterioration of their bodies or at least stop it by supplementing heavily.

Been so desperate in my health journey I'd try anything. I've been on all diets and even drank my urine.

V-9 COOK 6 hours: onions, garlic, mushrooms, celery, green leaves. asparagus, cabbage, cauliflower, broccoli.

Gravity works against you if you're eating inferior food. Things like eye-bags for example reflect poor fuel.

FEMINIST FRIGHT

FEMALE MANAGES LOVELY HOMELIFE

Female manages the home, creates a framework of regimens/priorities, makes things nice for you and me.

I cleaned his room and ordered everything around then I fixed veggie soup and that's how I show my love.

Alacrity, elasticity: everything now runs smoothly cuz we learned the huge trick of vegetable soups daily.

Depression, anxiety, loneliness, isolation: that's the vegan diet after honeymoon just like all extremism.

As a vegan I was so depressed, paranoid, isolated and touchy but dreamed of fats, salt, pot roasts, gravy.

After decades as a vegan the desire for salty fats, gravies and meats was so overwhelming I lost sleep.

Now I'm no longer vegan and a moderate mixed eater these cravings are gone and I eat to get the job done.

Not giving in to eat what I wanted and needed created mental illness, weakness, demoralization, wackiness.

My many years of vegan orthorexia are a perfect example of self-discipline creating mental illness.

I wanted animal fat and protein so bad and denied it out of the strength of Samson only to lose stamina.

All vegans eat is inflammation-inducing toxic garbage filled with oxalates, goitrogens and lectins.

Veggie soups were great but I'm still sleepy!   They didn't hurt nor help me really but will use some days.

FASTING VS. BACON ARGUMENTS

FEMINIST FRIGHT

Sometimes I wonder about myself: Do I have tenuous health or am I hypochondriacal as hell?

Where there are intrusive memories there are panic attacks and then, horrors, breathlessness.

Your body wants the fun of not having to digest the stuff. A call to fast is body pleading with us.

Gotta get the bacon. Will go on the thirty day challenge, nothing else. Greens and fruits are bad of course.

No more morning smoothies, just give me the bacon this vegan thing is BS and it's become obvious.

Why is **FAKE MEAT** everywhere? That's all they're buying/eating and it's cuz they want the real fare.

FAKE MEATS with tofu, beans, rice, lotsa hot sauce and salad on the side. Low calorie = more fiber, oh my.

Vegans into processed vegan foods and fake meats is such a joke they'll even eat cookies like Oreos.

The concoctions these vegans "create" look like a hodgepodge of sludge and it really makes me sick.

We were also told to drink water all day--what bull too! Water washes away the fats making you beautiful.

Modern paradox in dietary science: Greens with highest micronutrients (kale, spinach) are most dangerous.

We don't need greenhouses we need many freezers for the bacon.

Prescription: Eliminate the plants, eat your meat and wait. Daphne Reloaded

The relation between sugar and fat has always been reciprocal: the more sugar the less fat and visa versa.

FEMINIST FRIGHT

Humans have a natural desire to eat fat but when you take it out of the diet they'll replace it with sugar.
[It's ok, we simply re-adapt from fat-adaptation to glucose adaptation]

THE VISCIOUS VEIL OF VEGANISM

Veganism is a beautiful armor but makes for the heaviest sword. Daphne Reloaded

Who would want to eat a green leaf? Ray went to get the bacon so my headache will leave.

I don't care if there are carbs in melons. Gonna tweak things my way by instinct alone.

The diet of warm, fatty salty meats COMBINED with refreshing, succulent and sweet melons later on.

Bacon, salmon and melons is what we ended up on. 6 hour food window then fly, laugh, transcend, swoon.

They had their bacon and eggs in the morning: fat first--then it didn't matter if they ate again of course.

Salmon and lemon, bacon and melon: that's your shopping list for your new balanced diet of heaven.

Forget carbs and keto. Just enjoy your balanced life of melons and bacon, lemons and salmon.

As a hypersensitive you can't have grains, dairy, nightshades, citrus nuts/seeds or eggs. Just follow AIP.

After the fatty salty delicious bacon I obviously will want succulent melons later on. Now, come on.

Nothing could be more balanced than sweet succulent fruit and salty fatty bacon and forget greens hon'.

Forget grains poking holes in your gut then the fecal sludge ends up in your blood then on your face, yuk!

GREENS: OXALATES, GOITROGENS, LECTINS

Forget "dark greens" which are pure oxalates which hurt so much and cause blinding headaches.

Forget nightshades like tomato which cause leaky gut/blood sludge and end in heartburn all night.

Forget those dangerous vegetables causing goiters making you sick in self-defense so you won't eat em.

Forget those EGGS which smell like a sewer anyway. They aren't for you the Autoimmune Protocol says.

Watch the fruit too--too much sugar makes you old. Just some melon in the afternoon, nice and cold.

What's left? Bacon grease. Salmon on other days and in the afternoon cherries or cantaloupe please.

Forget citrus which is torture as ACID burns your insides, except a little lemon on your salmon's all right.

We live on glucose [sugar] yet can re-adapt to living on fat but I don't wanna live on meat, dairy, etc.

I'm back to low calorie just as I was as a teen. That means no fats: just fruits/greens/starches it seems.

Forget all dieting and say when you get up in the morning: What do I want to eat today? Then eat that.

100 KAREN KELLOCK BOOKS

AFFINITY OR MISERY
AGELESS CORNUCOPIA
AMERICA AWAKE!
AMERICA'S DAFT ERA
ARTS OF PALEO FASTING
AUTOPHAGY ON CHEATERS
BACKSTABBING NEUROTICS
BETRAYAL TRAUMA
BOOMERS AND BROKENNESS
BOOT ON NECK
CHAMPION GUIDES
COMMIE NUTHOUSE
COMMIES
COMMUNIST SPIRIT
CONTAGION OF MADNESS
CONTAGIOUS MADNESS
CULTURE CLASH BASHED
DAFT LEFT
DAILY FASTARIAN
DAM RATS
DIVERSITY IS CRUELTY
E-RACE WHITE
EVIL FREAKS (Beyond Gross)
THE END OR A BEND?
FEMALE BULLIES AND FEMI-NAZIS
FEMALE CARNALITY
FEMALE DUMB DOWN
FEMALE POWER DRIVE
FEMINISM AND RUIN 1 & 2
FIX FOR MISFITS
FOOLS & TRAMPS
FREEDOM SPEAKING
FRENEMY ENABLER
FRENEMY LIAR
FRENEMY THIEF
FRENEMY TRAITOR
TRENEMY TYRANT
GENIUS IS HELD DOWN
GLOBALISLAM
GOD USES THE FLAWED
HAZE OF THE LATTER DAYS

KAREN KELLOCK PH.D.

M.S. Political Science, San Diego State. Ph.D. in Psychology, University of California Irvine. Postdoctoral: UCI School of Medicine, Dept. of Psychiatry [NIMH Grants]. Developed the Debris Theory of Disease, a theory of system pathology in 120 books and 22 textbooks for the general public. The theory has a general formula: All disease is obstruction, all recovery is elimination, all success is attraction. The three obstructions are people, habit and food. Remove obstruction and snap to your goals, waiting in the wings.